Throwing My Boomerang

By Angelique McCabe

Library For All Ltd.

I0163063

LIBRARY FOR ALL

DIGITAL EDUCATION · FOR THE WORLD

Library For All is an Australian not for profit organisation with a mission to make knowledge accessible to all via an innovative digital library solution. Visit us at libraryforall.org

Throwing My Boomerang

First published 2023

Published by Library For All Ltd
Email: info@libraryforall.org
URL: libraryforall.org

This work is licensed under the Creative Commons Attribution-NonCommercial-NoDerivatives 4.0 International License. To view a copy of this license, visit http://creativecommons.org/licenses/by-nc-nd/4.0/.

Our Yarning logo design by Jason Lee, Bidjipidji Art

Original illustrations by John Robert Azuelo

Throwing My Boomerang
McCabe, Angelique
ISBN: 978-1-923063-01-3
SKU03364

Throwing My Boomerang

We respect and honour Aboriginal and Torres Strait Islander Elders past, present and future. We acknowledge the stories, traditions and living cultures of Aboriginal and Torres Strait Islander peoples on this land and commit to building a brighter future together.

Boomerangs are usually used for hunting by boys, like my dad and brother.

But I am learning to use one for fun, so that I can play games with my family.

4

I have tried and tried and tried.

But my arm is getting tired.

8

When I throw my boomerang,
it hits the ground with a great,
big bang!

My brother can throw his boomerang, my cousin can throw hers too.

But when I tried to throw mine,
it fell into some kangaroo poo.

"What's wrong?" Dad asked me.

He said I looked sad.

"My boomerang won't come back, it's really, really bad."

"Don't worry!" Dad said.
"It's time to go to bed."

"In the morning, I'll teach you how to throw your boomerang up high, over your head!"

We acknowledge the traditional and contemporary uses of boomerangs in Aboriginal culture being primarily for hunting by boys and men.

This story is a contemporary narrative written from the author's experience and perspective. This story is not to disrespect historical and cultural uses of the boomerang.

You can use these questions to talk about this book with your family, friends and teachers.

What did you learn from this book?

Describe this book in one word. Funny? Scary? Colourful? Interesting?

How did this book make you feel when you finished reading it?

What was your favourite part of this book?

download our reader app
getlibraryforall.org

About the author

Angelique McCabe was born on Murramarang land of the Yuin Nation and is a proud Wiradjuri woman. Angelique lives in Canberra on Ngunnawal land.

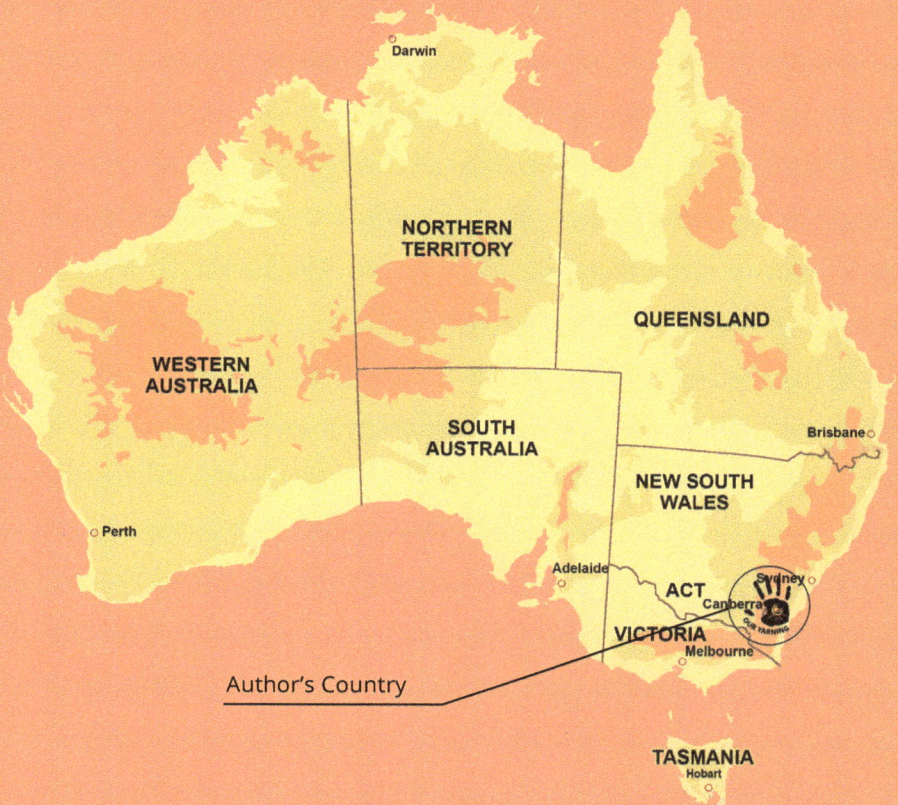

Darwin

NORTHERN
TERRITORY

QUEENSLAND

WESTERN
AUSTRALIA

SOUTH
AUSTRALIA

Brisbane

NEW SOUTH
WALES

Perth

Adelaide

Sydney

ACT

Canberra

VICTORIA

Melbourne

Author's Country

TASMANIA
Hobart

Our Yarning

Want to discover more books from this collection? Our Yarning is a collection of books written by Aboriginal and Torres Strait Islander peoples across Australia.

We know that children learn better, and enjoy reading more, when they see themselves in the stories, characters and illustrations of the books they read.

To download the app, visit the Google Play Store on any Android device and search 'Our Yarning'.

www.ingramcontent.com/pod-product-compliance
Lightning Source LLC
Chambersburg PA
CBHW042342040426
42448CB00019B/3378

9 781923 063013